FANTASTIC WORLD

MAMMALS

FANTASTIC WORLD

MAMMALS

STEVE PARKER &
MARTIN WALTERS

MiLes
KeLLy
PUBLISHING

First published in 2001 by Miles Kelly Publishing Ltd
(Originally published in hardback edition 2000)
Bardfield Centre
Great Bardfield
Essex CM7 4SL

24681097531

www.mileskelly.net
email: info@mileskelly.net

ISBN 1-84236-070-1

Design Jo Brewer
Page Make-up Helen Weller
Editor Steve Parker
Production Dawn Jones
Research & Index Jane Parker

Art Director Clare Sleven
Editorial Director Paula Borton
Director Jim Miles

The publishers wish to thank Ted Smart
for the generous loan of his illustrations.
Illustrators include Jim Channell, John Francis,
George Fryer and Robert Morton.

Printed in China

Contents

World of mammals — 6

Babies in pouches – *marsupials (pouched mammals)* — 8

Small, busy insect-eaters – *insect-eating mammals* — 10

Secret squeakers of darkness – *bats* — 12

Our constant cousins – *rats and mice* — 14

Gnawers of the Americas – *rodents of the Americas* — 16

Sharp claws and bushy tails – *squirrels and beavers* — 18

Long-eared, long-legged leapers – *rabbits, hares and pikas* — 20

Long-tongued ant-lickers – *anteaters, armadillos and pangolins* — 22

Close cousins, big and small – *elephants and their cousins* — 24

Thundering hooves on the plains – *horses, asses and zebras* — 26

Prehistoric 'pigs' of the forest – *tapirs* — 28

Edging towards extinction? – *rhinoceroses* — 30

Tall and slim, big and fat – *giraffes and hippos* — 32

High and dry in heat and cold – *camels and llamas* — 34

Fast, elegant plains-dwellers – *antelopes* — 36

The supreme hunters – *big cats* — 38

Lords of the jungle – *tigers* — 40

Growls and howls in the wilderness – *wolves, dogs and foxes* — 42

Far from cute and cuddly – *bears* — 44

Scampering through the trees – *raccoons and pandas* — 46

Slinky killers – *polecats, otters and badgers* — 48

Clever cat-like killers – *civets and genets* — 50

Superb swimmers of colder seas – *seals* — 52

Mysterious whales of the deep – *beaked whales* — 54

The greatest creatures on Earth – *great whales* — 56

Huge eyes in the dark forest – *bushbabies, pottos, lories and tarsiers* — 58

Monkeys with dog-like faces – *old world monkeys* — 60

Our closest cousins – *greater and lesser apes* — 62

Index — 64

World of mammals

▶ Within the pages of this book all the animals shown in the main picture are listed in this panel. They are named in alphabetical order.

6

Tiger
All (or most) of the animals pictured in this book have their own entries, giving important details about their lifestyles, where they live, what they eat and how they breed.

Mammals affect our lives in so many ways. We love to be scared by wild and fierce wolves, lions, bears and rhinos (provided we are quite safe from them). We like to imagine playing with dolphins or cuddling baby chimps. But what about the strange, secret lives of sloths in the rainforest, bats in the darkness and whales in the deepest sea? This book has them all.

Some of our most annoying pests are mammals, like mice and rats which ruin our foods. Yet our most valuable beasts of burden are donkeys, camels and elephants. And some of our best friends are dogs, cats, guinea pigs and ponies. This book shows all of these mammals – and many more.

A few mammals are well known. Shrews are tiny, cheetahs are fast, giant pandas are rare and blue whales are gigantic. But what about wambengers,

You will always find a strange or amazing fact in this panel!

gerenuks, linsangs, tamanduas, rock hyraxes and solenodons? This book uncovers their identities.

Mammals are warm-blooded, hairy or furry, and feed their babies on milk. (Just like us.) They live worldwide from poles to equator, and in all habitats from rainforest to desert. They even span the alphabet from aardvark to zebra. This book includes them all. It also explains how, in the modern world, more than a few mammals need our help.

Babies in pouches

▶ Brush-tailed phascogale (common wambenger)
▶ Hairy-nosed wombat
▶ Numbat (banded anteater)
▶ Quokka
▶ Red kangaroo
▶ Red-legged pademelon
▶ Tasmanian devil
▶ Yellow-footed rock wallaby

8

There are about 4080 kinds or species of mammals. Some 270 are marsupials – pouched mammals, named after the marsupium, a pocket or pouch on the front of the female's body. Marsupial babies are born at a very early stage of development, tiny and furless, eyes closed and limbs hardly developed. They wriggle to the mother's pouch where they stay, feed on her milk, grow and develop. Gradually the young marsupials begin to leave the pouch for short periods, although they still return for milk and safety. Marsupials live mainly in the Australian region, with some in South America and the Virginia opossum ranging into North America.

Yellow-footed rock wallaby
This tough wallaby lives in dry, rocky scrub in Central Australia. It eats almost any type of plant and leaps nimbly among the crags.

Tasmanian devil
The 'devil' is a small marsupial version of the hyaena. Active at night, it hunts small animals and scavenges on the carcasses of larger ones.

Red-legged pademelon
Pademelons are types of heavily built kangaroos which live in forests. The red-legged pademelon is small, with a head and body only 60 cm long. It lives mainly in damp woodlands along the east coast of Australia, foraging for leaves, shoots and similar soft plant food.

Red kangaroo
The largest of all marsupials, at 1.8 m tall and 80 kg in weight, only the male or 'boomer' is rusty-red. The female is smaller and known as the 'blue flier' due to her grey-blue fur.

Quokka
One of the smaller wallabies, the quokka is 50 cm long with a 30-cm tail. It is found in south-west Australia and eats plants. It has also taken to scavenging from rubbish tips.

Brush-tailed phascogale
There are marsupial versions of many types of mammals. The phascogales are like marsupial squirrels. They are widespread across Australia and have strong gnawing front teeth. Unlike real squirrels they eat small animals such as mice, birds and their eggs, insects and also honey.

Numbat
In south-west Australia the numbat is like a marsupial anteater. It has a sticky 10-cm tongue and licks up ants, termites and similar tiny food.

Hairy-nosed wombat
Wombats are like marsupial badgers. They live in large tunnel networks and emerge to eat shoots, roots, fruits and other plant food.

A hungry numbat can eat about 20,000 ants in one day.
A red kangaroo can bound along at 50 km/h.

Marsupials (pouched mammals)

Small, busy insect-eaters

- European hedgehog
- European mole
- Hispaniolan solenodon
- Pygmy shrew (least shrew)
- Pyrenean desman
- Rufous elephant shrew

Shrews, hedgehogs, moles and similar animals are known as insectivores. This name means 'insect-eaters' but many of these small, busy, active, darting mammals feed on a variety of tiny prey including worms, snails, slugs and spiders. There are about 345 kinds (species) of insectivores around the world. They include tenrecs, moonrats and desmans – as well as over 200 types of shrews, from giants to pygmies! Most insect-eaters have long, pointed, quivering, whiskery noses, little eyes and ears, and very sharp teeth. They are mainly active at night and they use their keen senses of smell and touch, rather than sight, to catch their prey.

Pygmy shrew
Pygmy shrews are the smallest of all land mammals, weighing only 2 g and measuring hardly 6 cm long – including the tail! They are fierce hunters and feed on worms five times their size, as well as insects. They are so small and active, and use up so much energy, that they must feed every 4–6 hours – or starve!

Hispaniolan solenodon
Solenodons look like rat-sized giant shrews. There are only two kinds, found in the Caribbean, and both are very rare. They use their very flexible snouts to sniff out insects from cracks and crevices. They can also pounce on larger prey like lizards and mice using their long, sharp claws.

Rufous elephant shrew
Elephant shrews were thought to be shrews, but they are so unusual that they are now put in their own mammal group. They run swiftly to escape predators along special pathways which they keep clear by regularly removing twigs and leaves. Their large eyes give them keen vision even in dark forests.

European hedgehog
These familiar garden predators feed mainly on worms, slugs and caterpillars. They are usually helpful to the gardener but they may be poisoned by eating slugs which have fed on slug pellets. Rolling into a tight, prickly ball protects the hedgehog from predators like foxes and stoats.

Pyrenean desman
The desman is like a water-living mole with a longer nose and a flattened tail. It has waterproof fur and webbed feet and swims very fast after small fish, tadpoles, pond snails and water insects. There are only two kinds of desman, one in the Pyrenees between France and Spain and the other in Asia.

European mole
A mole is seldom seen unless floods drive it to the surface. It spends most of its life in its large burrow network, feeding on worms, grubs and other soil creatures. The mole's front feet are almost like shovels to push aside earth. Molehills are loose soil that the mole thrusts up from its tunnels – which stretch up to 150 m.

The prickles of a hedgehog are specially thick, hardened, pointed hairs.
A fully grown hedgehog has about 16,000 of them.

Insect-eating mammals

Secret squeakers of darkness

▶ African yellow-winged bat
▶ Hammer-headed bat (horse-headed bat)
▶ Hoary bat
▶ Lesser horseshoe bat
▶ Long-eared bat
▶ Mexican fishing bat
▶ Noctule bat
▶ Red bat
▶ Spotted bat

Few people see bats. They fly at night, mostly in dense forests. Yet of the 4080 or so species of mammals, nearly one in four is a bat. Bats are found in all but the coldest parts of the world. Most are hand-sized and feed on small flying creatures such as moths. However some catch birds, mice or even fish. The large day-active bats known as flying foxes feed on fruit. The bat's arms are wings consisting of thin skin stretched between the enormously long hand and finger bones. A bat finds its way in darkness by making high-pitched clicks and squeaks and listening to the echoes which bounce back off nearby objects. This is called sonar or echolocation.

Noctule bat
The noctule is one of the largest European bats. It flies high, fast and straight as it hunts for insects. It also migrates up to 1500 km between its summer and winter homes.

Hammer-headed bat
A bat of tropical Africa, only males have the donkey-like nose. More than one hundred males may gather and fly in a swarm to attract females at breeding time.

African yellow-winged bat
This large bat has huge ears and yellow or orange wings. It hunts from a perch by day and night, and eats reptiles, birds and fish in addition to insects and spiders.

Mexican fishing bat
This bat detects the ripples made by a rising fish. It then swoops low over the water surface and hooks the fish in its long, sharp claws.

Long-eared bat
The big ears help to collect squeaky echoes as this bat navigates through woods in the dark. It is a skilled hunter of night-flying insects such as moths.

Hoary bat
The hoary bat is a fast and powerful flier. It has spread from mainland America to the Hawaiian Islands in the Pacific, helped by following winds.

Red bat
Most mother bats have one or at most two babies. The red bat often has three. Like many other bat species, red bats hibernate inside hollow trees.

Lesser horseshoe bat
Horseshoe bats are named after the U-shaped folds of skin around the nose, which help to direct their high-pitched (ultrasonic) squeaks.

Spotted bat
This bat is found in Mexico and the southern states of the USA. Like many bat species it is a communal rooster – it gathers in groups or colonies to rest.

The Mexican free-tailed bat forms the largest colonies of any bat (and of almost any animal). As many as 10 million may cluster together in a single cave.

Our constant cousins

- African pygmy mouse
- Black rat
- Brown rat (Norway or water rat)
- Spiny mouse
- Desert jerboa
- Harvest mouse
- House mouse
- Rock mouse
- Striped field mouse
- Three-toed jerboa
- Wood mouse
- Yellow-necked field mouse

14

It is said that, wherever you are in the world, you are never more than a few metres away from a mouse or rat – perhaps even at sea! There are well over 1200 different kinds, or species, of these rodents so they make up by far the largest group of mammals. Many of them are small, quick and adaptable and have taken to living near people. They eat our stores of grains and food in our cupboards and larders, just as they feed on seeds, nuts and berries in the wild. Rats and mice have long, sharp front teeth to chew and gnaw even the hardest items. Some mice are as small as your thumb. The largest rats are almost the size of pet cats.

House mouse
House mice have lived in buildings and 'shared' our food for thousands of years. They breed quickly too. A female can produce 25 young in six months.

African pygmy mouse
The pygmy mouse lives in grassland and scrub in East Africa. It is one of the smallest mice, measuring just 10 cm in total length.

Striped field mouse
Unlike most mice, this striped species eats few green plants. It feeds on seeds and fruits and also catches insects, worms and slugs.

Harvest mouse
An expert climber, this tiny mouse uses its long, grasping tail to clamber among grass stems. It lives in a tennis-ball-sized nest of woven stalks.

Desert jerboa
Jerboas are like tiny kangaroos. They make huge leaps using their long back legs, balanced by the long tail. They live in African and Asian deserts.

Rock mouse
This large mouse lives in dry, rocky places and makes its nest in a safe crevice. Its long whiskers help it to feel its way among the stones at night.

Yellow-necked field mouse
This agile mouse is common across Europe. It lives mainly in woods, fields and gardens. Like many mice it is active at night with big, beady eyes to see in the dark.

Brown rat
The brown rat lives almost everywhere, including farms, gardens, rubbish dumps, city centres, ditches and even sewers. It is an excellent swimmer and sometimes called the 'water rat'.

Black rat
Black rats live mainly in warmer regions. They are also called ship rats because they can climb mooring ropes into boats and also swim well. They carry diseases such as plague.

Some jerboas can jump 3 m – equivalent to a person leaping six times the human long-jump world record.

Gnawers of the Americas

▸ Capybara
▸ Cavy (wild guinea pig)
▸ Chinchilla
▸ Coypu
▸ Crested porcupine
▸ Hutia
▸ North American porcupine
▸ South American porcupine

Rodents vary from pygmy voles and pocket mice to rats, squirrels and beavers. Most bigger rodents live in the Americas, like the largest of them all, the capybara. The key feature of a rodent is its teeth. It has four big incisor teeth at the very front of the mouth, two in the upper jaw and two in the lower. They are shaped like chisels or spades with wide, sharp, straight ends. They never stop growing and if the owner never gnawed they would eventually pierce the inside of its mouth. However they are continually worn down as the creature bites, gnashes, nips and nibbles at tough plant food such as roots, twigs, bark, seeds and nuts.

16

Cavy
This is the original 'guinea pig' from which our many kinds of pet guinea pigs are bred. It lives in grassy and rocky scrub in southern South America.

Coypu
Coypus swim well and dig long riverbank burrows with their webbed feet. Originally from southern South America, they have escaped from fur farms in other regions such as Europe.

North American porcupine
Porcupines move with a slow, shuffling waddle. They need not run from enemies since they are protected by long, sharp spines.

Hutia
Hutias are rare rodents of the West Indies. They eat plants and also small animals like snails and lizards, climbing after them through the trees.

Crested porcupine
This porcupine has extra-big spines or quills up to 30 cm long on its back. Like most other porcupines it eats fruits, leaves, buds and similar plant food.

South American porcupine
Gripping the branches with its curly grasping tail and sharp-clawed toes, this porcupine is quite at home in trees.

Chinchilla
Chinchillas live on the rocky slopes of the southern Andes Mountains. Fast and agile, they leap on their strong back legs as they look for food to hold in their front paws and nibble. At night they sleep in groups of 50 or more, in holes among the rocks. Their long, soft fur and bushy tails keep them warm.

Capybara
Almost as big as a small pony, the capybara is never far from water. If a jaguar comes near the capybara can stay under the surface for five minutes – but then it might be grabbed by a crocodile! These huge rodents live in groups of 10–40 in the Amazon region. They feed on all kinds of grasses and water plants.

Porcupines cannot shoot out their quills as some tales suggest.
But the quills have barbed tips and work their way deep into an attacker's body.

Rodents of the Americas

Sharp claws and bushy tails

▶ African bush squirrel
▶ Asiatic striped palm squirrel
▶ Beaver
▶ Bush-tailed ground squirrel
▶ Common marmot
▶ Eurasian red squirrel
▶ Malabar giant squirrel (Indian giant squirrel)
▶ Northern flying squirrel

Not all squirrels are bright-eyed, bushy-tailed and live in trees. But most are. The squirrel family has nearly 270 members and is part of the vast rodent group of mammals. As well as typical tree-dwelling squirrels it includes the bigger, heavier marmots, and also ground squirrels such as prairie dogs and chipmunks which burrow in soil. However most squirrels are amazing climbers, clinging to the bark with their sharp claws and then making huge leaps, using their furry tails for balance and steering in mid air. Flying squirrels have taken this a stage further and swoop between trees using parachute-like flaps of stretched skin along the sides of the body.

Common marmot
Marmots are like big ground squirrels, thick-set and thick-furred with short tails. They live in high meadows and rocky scrub.

African bush squirrel
This slim, grey, rather rat-like squirrel lives in the Congo region of West and Central Africa. It is at home in trees or on the ground.

Beaver
Beavers are not squirrels but close rodent relations. They grow up to 1.5 m long including the scaly tail, which is slapped on the water to warn other family members of danger. Beavers swim well with their webbed back feet. They fell trees by gnawing, for food and to build a dam which makes a home pool.

Eurasian red squirrel
With its bright fur and neat ear tufts, the red squirrel is very distinctive. It sometimes buries seeds and nuts, and sniffs them out later in the year from deep in the soil.

Asiatic striped palm squirrel
These squirrels are found mainly in Sri Lanka and India. They resemble chipmunks and are always active, searching the forest edge for buds, nuts and seeds.

Malabar giant squirrel
This is a very bulky squirrel, weighing up to 3 kg. It often leans forwards from a branch to feed, back feet gripping firmly and balanced by its tail. This leaves its front feet free to grab food. Many squirrels hold items in their front paws as they eat, turning nuts to be cracked open with the teeth.

Northern flying squirrel
Flying squirrels live mainly in dense forests. Unlike most squirrels they tend to be active at night, seeing in the dark with their large eyes.

Bush-tailed ground squirrel
Ground squirrels and prairie dogs live in huge networks of burrows and tunnels. They disappear at once into these if danger appears.

One red squirrel may strip open more than 150 pine cones in a single day, to get at the pine nuts (seeds) between the cone's flap-like scales.

Squirrels and beavers

Long-eared, long-legged leapers

- Black-tailed jackrabbit
- Brown hare (common hare)
- Mountain hare (varying or tundra hare)
- Northern pika
- Rabbit (common or European rabbit, cony)
- Red pika
- Snowshoe hare
- Steppe pika

Rabbits and hares live in open, grassy country. With their huge ears, large eyes and twitching noses, they are always alert to danger and ready to escape into their burrows, hide in the undergrowth or race off at great speed. The rabbit itself has been taken to many parts of the world where it thrives – especially Australia. But introduced rabbits not only ruin farmland, they damage the balance of nature in wilderness areas. There are about 45 species in the group. Those with longer legs and longer ears are usually called hares (jackrabbits in North America). Pikas are small vole-like cousins of rabbits. They live mainly in Asia.

Mountain hare
This dappled hare lives mainly in the Arctic and mountain habitats. The more snow that falls in its region, the whiter its coat turns in winter.

Snowshoe hare
The hairy feet of this hare allow it to run over snow without sinking. It lives in the northern forests of North America and is a favourite prey of lynx.

Northern pika
Pikas are small creatures resembling voles or guinea pigs, with rounded ears and almost no tail. Like rabbits they feed mainly on grasses and other plants. Pikas 'hay-make', gathering grass stems into their burrows during the summer and autumn. They eat this food during the long winter.

Brown hare
Found in many parts of Europe and Asia, the brown hare can cover 3 m in one leap. However it only runs as a last resort, preferring to crouch still until danger has passed.

Black-tailed jackrabbit
This North American hare's huge ears detect very faint noises. They also give off heat and help the jackrabbit stay cool in the hot summer sun.

Rabbit
The common rabbit is all too common in many places. It came originally from Spain and North Africa but it has invaded many other countries, eating local plants so that other animals starve, as well as destroying crops and digging its home burrows, called warrens. The many types of pet rabbits are bred from it.

Red pika
Most pikas prefer rocky upland slopes. The red pika lives in the Tien Shan mountain range in central Asia, at heights of up to 4000 m.

Steppe pika
The steppe pika digs an elaborate network of burrows in the steppes or grasslands of Asia. It retreats underground to escape its many predators.

The brown hare can race along at speeds of up to 65 km/h.
Large-eared pikas live higher than almost any other mammal, 6000 m up in the Himalayas.

Rabbits, hares and pikas

Long-tongued ant-lickers

- Burmeister's armadillo
- Fairy armadillo
- Giant anteater
- Naked-tailed armadillo
- Nine-banded armadillo (common long-nosed armadillo)
- Pichi
- Silky anteater (two-toed anteater)
- Small-scaled tree pangolin
- Tamandua (tree or collared anteater)

22

Ants and termites fight and bite when caught. But they are so tiny that big ant-eating mammals such as anteaters, pangolins and armadillos have little to fear. They lick and pick up their miniature victims dozens at a time with their long sticky tongues.

Tamandua

Tamanduas are smaller, tree-living versions of the giant anteater. They can use the strong, flexible, furless tail to wrap around branches like a fifth foot. The tamandua can walk on the ground but it is slow, clumsy and at greater risk from predators. These anteaters live in the forests of Central and South America.

Giant anteater

The giant anteater is a very odd-looking mammal with its brush-like tail, shaggy fur and long, curved nose. It grows to 2 m long including the tail and shuffles through wood or scrub in Central and South America. It digs open a nest using its very long, sharp claws, laps up a few hundred insects and moves on.

Small-scaled tree pangolin

This is one of four African pangolins. The long, curving, prehensile (grasping) tail helps it to climb in the branches, using its sharp-edged scales to get an even better grip on the bark. Tree pangolins hunt at night for nests of ants and termites high in trees. They sleep in their own tree nests by day.

Silky anteater

This anteater has soft, golden fur like a cuddly toy. But it can slash out with its fearsome sharp, curved front claws. Also, like other anteaters, it does not destroy a nest while feeding. It makes a small hole, takes some occupants, then leaves the ants to multiply and repair their nest, so that they can be a future meal.

Nine-banded armadillo

Armadillos eat mainly ants, termites and other small creatures such as woodlice and worms. But some types, especially the nine-banded armadillo (opposite, shown lower right) are also fond of fruit. There are 20 species of armadillos living in South and Central America, with a few north to Mexico and the southern USA. They have very keen noses to detect food in the soil and strong front claws to dig rapidly for roots, termites and ants. Smallest is the fairy armadillo from southern South America (lower left) at only 15 cm long. It has less armour-plating and spends much time burrowing in sandy soil. Also shown are the naked-tailed armadillo (centre left), pichi (centre right) and the small Burmeister's armadillo (lower middle).

When feeding the giant anteater flicks its 60-cm-long tongue in and out twice every second.

Anteaters, armadillos and pangolins

Close cousins, big and small

▶ Aardvark
▶ African elephant
▶ Asian elephant
▶ Rock hyrax

The two kinds of elephants are the largest land animals in the world. They also come from a very ancient group of mammals. Various kinds of elephants and mammoths have lived on Earth for more than 30 million years. The elephant's trunk, which is really its very long nose and upper lip, is like a multi-purpose fifth limb. It can grasp and pull leaves and similar food into the mouth for chewing. It sucks up water and squirts it into the mouth when the elephant drinks. The trunk also sniffs the air for scents. Elephants live in small herds, usually of females and young. The trunk is very important for touching, stroking and smelling other herd members.

24

Asian elephant
Slightly smaller than the African elephant, the Asian elephant also has smaller ears and shorter tusks. The tusks are very large upper teeth called incisors. They are made of a hard white substance, ivory. The elephant uses them to dig for food and water and to defend itself against enemies such as tigers.

African elephant
A large male stands more than 3 m tall, has a head and body nearly 7 m long and weighs over 5 tonnes. The tusks grow through life. Cows (females) have tusks too but they are much smaller. The massive ears help the elephant to hear tiny sounds and they also work like flapping fans to keep its bulky body cool. An elephant eats about 150 kg of food each day – the weight of two adult people. It includes grasses, leaves from trees and also twigs, bark and roots. An elephant herd is led by one or two experienced older females called matriarchs who know where to find food and water. Young males form groups known as bachelor herds. Old males or 'tuskers' usually live alone.

Aardvark
The name *aardvark* means 'earth pig' in the Swahili language of Africa. But this curious creature, about 2 m long from nose to tail, is not a type of pig. In fact it is not like any other mammal, although its closest cousins are probably the elephants. Like these giant relatives, the aardvark belongs to a very ancient group of mammals and it lives on the African savannah (grasslands). It comes out at night to search for its food of ants and termites, which it licks up with its long, sticky tongue. The aardvark has only a few weak teeth and does not chew. Its tiny prey are ground up in its strong, muscular stomach. Aardvarks travel 20 km or more each night for food. They live alone in deep burrows up to 15 m long.

Rock hyrax
Hyraxes (hyraces) look like large rats or small bears. But they are a separate group of mammals – and the closest living cousins of the elephants. Rock hyraxes eat grasses and similar plants. They live in groups in the drier parts of Africa, especially on inland cliffs and among the rocky outcrops known as kopjes.

An old bull (male) African elephant may be over 70 years of age and have tusks 3 m in length.

Elephants and their cousins

Thundering hooves on the plains

▶ African wild ass
▶ Asiatic wild ass
▶ Chapman's zebra
▶ Donkey
▶ Grevy's zebra
▶ Mountain zebra
▶ Plains zebra (common or Burchell's zebra)
▶ Przewalski's horse

If wild horses, asses and zebras were all the same colour, they would be very difficult to tell apart. They are all hoofed mammals, or ungulates, and close cousins of rhinos and tapirs. They are built for grazing on grasses and other low plants, and for galloping at high speed for long distances across open country. The rare Przewalski's horse of the Mongolian steppes (grasslands) is probably similar to the ancestor of today's many domestic horse breeds. Wild asses are smaller than most horses and have longer ears, less even manes and tufted tails. Zebras live mainly on the savannahs of East and Southern Africa.

26

Grevy's zebra
Grevy's zebras live mainly in north-east Africa, especially Ethiopia and Somalia, where the land is dry, rocky, scrubby and almost desert-like. Grevy's is the largest of the three kinds (species) of zebras, with a head and body about 2.8 m long and a weight of 400 kg. Its narrow vertical stripes are more black than white.

Plains zebra
Zebras spend much of the day grazing, on the lookout for lions, hyaenas and African wild dogs. They live in small groups of a stallion (male) with 5–10 mares (females) and their foals (young).

Przewalski's horse
This wild horse was rescued from extinction by breeding in captivity. It stands only 1.3 m tall. Unlike a domesticated horse it has a stiff, upright mane.

Chapman's zebra
This is a darker variety of the plains zebra, with faint lines between the main stripes. Zebras gather in huge herds to find new grass.

Mountain zebra
The smallest and rarest zebra lives in the mountainous grasslands of south-west Africa. It has a slim build with narrow black stripes and a white belly.

Asiatic wild ass
Mainly a desert dweller, this ass ranges from northern India and Tibet west to Iran and Syria. It is larger and more horse-like than the African wild ass and has a browner coat, but it lives in small family herds like its cousin. There are various local names for different varieties such as the onager and kiang.

African wild ass
Found in north-east Africa, this ass is very like its descendant, the donkey. There may be a dark shoulder line or faint zebra-type leg stripes.

Donkey
The donkey is a domesticated form of the African wild ass. It is usually grey but some are brown, as shown in this breed called the Spanish giant donkey.

Przewalski's horses disappeared from their natural wild home of Central Asia in the 1960s. Hopefully captive-bred members released there will thrive again in the wild.

Horses, asses and zebras

Prehistoric 'pigs' of the forest

▶ Baird's tapir
▶ Brazilian (South American or lowland) tapir – adult
▶ Brazilian tapir – young
▶ Malaysian tapir – adult
▶ Malaysian tapir – young
▶ Mountain (woolly or Andean) tapir

Tapirs are something of a leftover from the prehistoric age. Fossil remains of their bones and teeth show that the tapirs roaming forests more than 25 million years ago were hardly different from today's versions. These creatures resemble pigs but they are close cousins of rhinos. They eat plants and live mainly in woods and forests. There are four kinds or species, all shown here. Largest is Baird's tapir, but only just. A typical tapir has a head and body about 2 m long, a small tail of up to 10 cm, and stands around 100 cm tall at the shoulder. It is a strong, sturdy, thick-set animal that weighs 250 kg or more – as much as four adult people!

28

Brazilian tapir

This is the widest ranging type, found across the northern half of South America. It is also the only tapir that lives in grassy plains as well as forests. Like the others it feeds at night and eats all kinds of plant food such as leaves, grasses, stems, buds, shoots, flowers and fruits. Sometimes it raids corn and other farm crops.

Baird's tapir

This tapir has a neck mane of stiff, bristly hairs. It is found from Mexico down to northern South America. Like other tapirs in the region its main enemy is South America's big cat – the jaguar. If a tapir is attacked it bites hard, kicks even harder, thrashes about and then crashes off through the thick undergrowth.

Malaysian tapir

This is the only tapir not from South America. It's from – Malaysia! Also Thailand and other parts of Southeast Asia. Its striking black and white pattern probably helps with camouflage in its dense rainforest home. It breaks up its body outline and recognizable pig-like shape. All tapirs are excellent swimmers.

Young Brazilian tapir

Tapirs live alone except for a mother with her baby, or when male and female come together for a day or two to mate. This happens at any time of year. The baby is born 13 months later in a nest or den deep in the forest. It hides here, staying perfectly still, while the mother goes off to feed.

Mountain tapir

Forests up to 4500 m high on the massive Andes Mountains are home to this tapir. It is well protected against the night cold by its long, woolly coat. Despite its clumsy appearance, it can easily climb steep slopes and scramble over loose rocks. A tapir's eyesight is not so keen and it finds food mainly by smell.

Young Malaysian tapir

Very different from its parents, this baby tapir has a red-brown coat with white spots and stripes. The pattern helps to conceal it in the forest's dappled shade. After two months the pattern begins to fade. By six months old the youngster is black and white and almost ready to leave its mother.

Tapirs have four toes on each front foot but only three on each back foot.

Edging towards extinction?

▶ Black rhino (hook-lipped rhinoceros)

▶ Indian rhino (greater one-horned rhinoceros)

▶ Javan rhino (lesser one-horned rhinoceros)

▶ Sumatran rhino (Asian two-horned rhinoceros)

▶ White rhino (square-lipped rhinoceros)

Rhinos look like hippos or elephants, but they are close relatives of tapirs and horses. These massive hoofed creatures are the tanks of the animal world, with extremely thick skin, bulky bodies and the long horn (or horns) on the nose. Both male and female have horns. A rhino has small eyes and sees poorly. But its hearing is very good, the large ears swivelling to pick up distant sounds, and its nose is even more sensitive. All five kinds or species of rhinos are threatened, mainly by loss of their natural habitat. But they are still hunted for their horns. The horn may be made into a dagger handle or ground up as a medicine (even though it has no healing effect).

Javan rhino

This is the rarest rhino and one of the world's most threatened animals. It is now found only in wildlife reserves in the west of the island of Java, where its population numbers tens rather than hundreds. Its main habitats are rainforests but these are being felled for timber and to make way for farmland.

Sumatran rhino

The Sumatran rhino of Southeast Asia has two horns, like the two African types. It is the smallest rhino, up to 3 m in head-body length and 750 kg in weight. It also differs from other rhinos because it is partly covered in long hair. It is a rare rainforest animal, with a total number of only 100–200.

Indian rhino

The Indian rhino prefers open scrub and grassland to forests. Its heavy skin, almost 2 cm thick, is divided into distinct plates which give it a suit-of-armour appearance. Also the lumps in the skin make it look as if it has been bolted on! The 1500 or so surviving Indian rhinos live mainly in Bengal, Assam and Nepal.

White rhino

The largest rhino reaches a length of 4.2 m, with a shoulder height of 1.9 m and a weight of 3.5 tonnes. The 'white' does not refer to the colour, which is pale grey. It means 'wide' from this rhino's broad, squared-off snout. White rhinos live in dry bush and grassland across Africa, especially in the south.

Black rhino

Black rhinos, which are actually grey-brown, range widely across Africa. But they have suffered badly from the traps and guns of poachers, being completely wiped out in some areas. The black rhino's long, flexible upper lip can grasp leaves and shoots as it browses on rainforest trees and scrubland bushes. This type of rhino is often active by night, unlike its relatives. Rhinos tend to live alone except for a mother with her baby. (White rhinos sometimes form small groups as they search for food.) One of the main problems facing all rhinos is that, like many large animals, they breed very slowly. The female usually has one young every two to four years. This means rhino numbers take a long time to build up.

Rhino horns are not made of real horn but of very tightly-packed hairs. The largest belonged to a white rhino and was more than 1.5 m long.

Rhinoceroses

Tall and slim, big and fat

▶ Baringo giraffe
▶ Hippo
  (hippopotamus)
▶ Masai giraffe
▶ Nubian giraffe
▶ Okapi
▶ Pygmy hippo
▶ Reticulated giraffe
▶ Transvaal giraffe

The giraffe is one of the most peculiar mammals, with its extremely long neck and its ungainly, stick-like legs. Giraffes are easy to spot in their favoured habitat, the open bush of Africa, where they use their height to reach tasty twigs and shoots almost 7 m above the ground. There is only one main kind or species of giraffe, but this includes several varieties each with a distinctive coat pattern. The rare okapi of West African forests is a close cousin of the giraffe. Hippos are also hoofed mammals, like giraffes and okapis. They spend much of the day almost submerged in rivers or lakes, and come out at night to graze on nearby grasses and other plants.

32

Okapi
The okapi is such a shy forest-dweller that it is seldom seen. It gathers leaves using its curly dark-blue tongue which is almost 50 cm long!

Hippo
Hippos often lie in the water with just their ears, eyes and nostrils visible at the surface. Each hippo herd occupies a stretch or territory of river. Male hippos sometimes fight each other for the territory or for females at breeding time. They can inflict nasty wounds on each other with their long, tusk-like teeth.

Pygmy hippo
This mini-hippo is only about 90 cm tall but it is just as tubby as its big cousin and weighs up to 250 kg. It is found in the swampy forests of West Africa but is very rare, with just a few thousand remaining. Pygmy hippos feed mainly on grasses, roots and shoots which they find by grubbing on the forest floor.

Giraffe
Giraffes are by far the tallest animals. An adult male can grow to almost 6 m. Although the neck is so long it has only seven neck bones inside, just like other mammals (and ourselves). The giraffe's tongue is about 45 cm long, tough and flexible, and used to twist twigs and leaves from even the thorniest trees.

Distinctive giraffe varieties include the reticulated giraffe (shown opposite in the centre, just behind the okapi), with large chestnut patches separated by thin white lines. The Masai giraffe (upper left) has irregular, often star-shaped patches. Also shown are the Baringo giraffe (upper centre), two Transvaal giraffes (upper right and middle right) and a Nubian giraffe (lower right). Each giraffe's coat pattern stays the same through its life.

The male hippo is the third-biggest land mammal after the two types of elephants.
It can be more than 4 m long and weigh well over 3 tonnes.

Giraffes and hippos

High and dry in heat and cold

▶ Alpaca
▶ Bactrian camel (Asian or two-humped camel)
▶ Dromedary (Arabian or one-humped camel)
▶ Guanaco
▶ Llama
▶ Vicuna

Camels are specialized for harsh habitats. The dromedary endures heat and drought in the deserts of North Africa, the Middle East and Australia. The Bactrian camel also survives drought – and the biting winter winds of the Gobi Desert. Most camels today are domesticated by people as beasts of burden and to provide milk, meat, wool and skins. However a few Bactrian herds still roam the Gobi, and dromedaries taken to Australia by people now run wild in the outback. Llamas and alpacas are South American versions of camels, living mainly along the Andes mountains. They are also domesticated. Their wild cousins are guanacos and vicunas.

34

Alpaca
Like woollier versions of the llama, some alpacas live wild at heights of up to 4800 m in the Andes. Also like llamas, alpacas have been domesticated, although mainly for their fine wool rather than as pack animals. They grow to about 100 cm tall at the shoulder and weigh 60 kg.

Vicuna
The vicuna is the smallest member of the camel group and lives at heights of up to 5500 m, where the air is very thin. Its numbers fell drastically through hunting for meat and its exceptionally fine woolly coat. Since protection in 1969 its numbers have risen to more than 100,000.

Guanaco
Once found in many parts of South America, the guanaco is now limited to Argentina. Like its relatives, it is highly prized for its fur. Guanacos are found in dry grasslands, shrublands and even in forests. They live in small herds of one male with several females and their young.

Bactrian camel
The Bactrian's thick fur helps to keep out the winter cold of the Mongolian high grasslands. The hump of a camel does not store water. It contains fat, which the camel can use as a food store when plants are scarce. However the fat can be broken down by the camel's special body chemistry to produce water too.

Llama
The llama is found in many regions of mountain grassland and scrub along the Andes. Like the camels it has a long history as a domesticated animal – for transport, as well as for its fur, milk and meat. Llamas have been taken to wildlife parks in many other continents and are also bred as large, pony-like pets.

Dromedary
There are now two breeds of this camel species. One is tall and strong, and still used as a pack animal in remote places where there are few roads. It seems to stride along slowly, but it can walk all day and cover 30 km even with a heavy load. The other breed is smaller and much slimmer and used for racing.

A camel can go for a week without water, then drink 50 litres in just a few minutes.

Camels and llamas

Fast, elegant plains-dwellers

▸ Blue wildebeest (brindled gnu or brindled wildebeest)
▸ Bontebok (blesbok)
▸ Gemsbok (Beisa oryx)
▸ Gerenuk
▸ Klipspringer
▸ Pronghorn
▸ Sable
▸ Scimitar oryx (white oryx)
▸ Topi (sassaby)

36

Antelopes have keen sight, excellent hearing and sensitive noses, and they can run, dodge, swerve and jink at great speed. This is just as well, because these mainly grazing mammals are at great risk from predators such as lions, cheetahs, leopards and wild dogs. Many antelopes live on the African savannah (grassland), gathering in large herds for safety in numbers. They wander in search of the rains which bring fresh grass. Unlike the antlers of deer, which are shed each year, the horns of an antelope grow through life. Horn length and shape vary – in gazelles and small antelopes they are short, while the sable and oryx have long, curved horns.

Blue wildebeest
This cow-like antelope is strong and sturdy rather than slim and speedy. It forms huge herds on regular migrations across the African savannahs.

Topi
Topi are at home in greener, more marshy regions of the open savannah. They gather into herds of 3000 or more and travel to fresh grazing.

Klipspringer
These dainty antelopes live in stony, rocky places and jump with great agility. Their hooves are small and rubbery to give a firm grip on the rock.

Scimitar oryx
Named after its sword-shaped curving horns, this antelope was once widespread in North Africa. It now lives in a small area near the Red Sea.

Sable
The sable antelope has extremely long horns, measuring more than 1.5 m around their graceful curve. It prefers damp grassland and open woods.

Pronghorn
The only antelope in America, the pronghorn inhabits open prairie. It is one of the fastest runners in the world and, unusually, sheds its horns yearly.

Bontebok
The purple-brown bontebok prefers open grassland in Southern Africa. In the 1930s it almost become extinct but wildlife protection laws have helped to increase its numbers.

Gemsbok
The gemsbok is a type of oryx. It lives in dry savannahs across large regions of East and Southern Africa. It stands 1.2 m tall at the shoulder and its horns can be more than 100 cm long.

Gerenuk
The graceful gerenuk balances on its back legs and stretches its long neck upwards to eat the foliage of trees and tall bushes. Only the male gerenuk has horns.

The pronghorn can run at up to 90 km/h and sustain this speed for many minutes, unlike its rival for fastest land animal, the cheetah.

Antelopes

The supreme hunters

▶ Cheetah
▶ Clouded leopard
▶ Jaguar
▶ Lion (male) and lioness (female)
▶ Snow leopard (ounce)

Big cats are the most fearsome hunters in the animal world. They stalk in stealthy silence, charge like lightning, pounce on prey with ferocious speed, stab the victim with their massive sharp teeth and slash with their cruel claws. The seven types of big cats are the tiger (see page 40), lion, cheetah, jaguar, leopard, snow leopard and clouded leopard. All are top predators in their habitats. However they sometimes come into conflict – for example, lions on the African plains sometimes kill and eat cheetah cubs. Cheetahs hunt mainly by day but the other big cats prowl mainly in twilight or at night. Lions live in groups called prides but all the others stalk alone.

Lion
The male lion's shaggy neck mane of thick fur makes him look even bigger and more ferocious. A typical pride of lions has 2–4 males. They patrol the pride's home area or territory, roar and leave urine scent-marks to keep out lions of other prides. They also defend the pride against threats such as hyaenas.

Clouded leopard
This is the smallest big cat, with a head and body about 80 cm long and a weight of 15–20 kg. It lives in thick forests from India across to Southeast Asia and spends most of its time in trees hunting birds, squirrels and monkeys. This leopard is such a good climber that it can run down trees head-first.

Cheetah
Famed as the fastest thing on four legs, the cheetah really does sprint at amazing speed. But usually for less than a minute since it has little endurance. Any longer and its prey, such as a Thomson's gazelle or impala, is likely to get away. Cheetahs live in dry, open areas in Africa, including the Sahara.

Lioness
Male lions rarely hunt. Catching food is the task of the lionesses, who are smaller and lack manes. They work as a team to surround and ambush prey such as zebras, antelopes and gazelles. Lions live in bush, scrub, grassland and woods across most of Africa. A few survive in the Gir Forest of north-west India.

Jaguar
The only big cat in South America, the jaguar likes water and swims very well. It creeps through swampy forests to hunt prey such as tapirs, peccaries, monkeys, turtles, fish, and rodents like capybaras. With the loss of forests due to farming and logging, some jaguars now live in rocky hills or dry scrubland.

Snow leopard
The long, thick fur of the snow leopard keeps it warm in the world's highest mountains – the Himalayas of Central Asia. Its paws are very wide and have fur between the sole pads to grip slippery ice. Snow leopards prey on a range of animals, from birds and rats to large wild cattle and sheep.

The cheetah can reach a top speed of about 100 km/h.
Its average chase when hunting is 150–200 m long and lasts about 20 seconds.

Big cats

Lords of the jungle

▶ Caspian tiger
▶ Indian tiger
▶ Siberian tiger
▶ Sumatran tiger
▶ White Indian tiger

Biggest of big cats, the tiger has inspired awe, respect and fear for thousands of years. It is a solitary, secretive, stealthy hunter of forest, scrub, long grass and tangled undergrowth known in India as jangle, *a term which was the origin of the word 'jungle'. All tigers belong to the same species,* Panthera tigris. *There are different varieties of this species across Asia. The Caspian tiger dwells to the east of the Caspian Sea, the Indian tiger in India and Bangladesh, the Indo-Chinese tiger on the mainland of Southeast Asia, and further varieties on large islands such as Sumatra and Java. Most massive and powerful is the great Siberian tiger of far East Asia.*

40

Caspian tiger
The most westerly variety, the Caspian tiger was found from Iran across southern Russia to western China. It is now very, very rare. Tigers hunt mainly large prey including various deer like sambar, chital, swamp and red deer, also wild pigs, gaur (wild cattle), water buffalo and even young rhino or elephants.

Sumatran tiger
One of the smaller varieties, the Sumatran tiger is about 2.5 m long from nose to tail and weighs up to 150 kg. It has a 'face ruff' of long cheek fur. Tigers are solitary – they usually live and hunt alone. If two tigers are together they are either a male and female at breeding time or a mother with her youngster.

Indian tiger
The Indian tiger is the most numerous variety yet it still numbers just a few thousand in the wild. Its main stronghold is the vast Sunderbans delta of mangrove swamps at the mouth of the River Ganges, on the India-Bangladesh border. Unlike many wild cats, tigers love water. They could lie in it all day – and do!

White Indian tiger
Most mammals produce very pale or very dark forms, which are born naturally from time to time of normal-coloured parents. The white tiger is a famous example and popular with zoos. It occurs mainly in north-east India and seems to survive just as well in the wild as its yellow-brown cousins.

Siberian tiger
The long, thick coat of the biggest tiger variety protects against the icy winds and thick snow of far eastern Russia and China. The Siberian tiger grows to more than 3.2 m from nose to tail. It is also more muscular and sturdy than other varieties, weighing over 320 kg. There are probably less than 200 left.

TIGER CONSERVATION
Rarely a tiger is killed because it keeps attacking cattle or humans. But tigers are also killed illegally for their body parts. For example, ground-up tiger bones are supposed to have mysterious powers to heal sick people. Medical tests show that there are no such powers. But still the poachers kill tigers.

A tiger is not especially brave against other animals. It is sometimes driven from its kill by a hungry hyaena or even a determined jackal.

Tigers

Growls and howls in the wilderness

- African wild dog (Cape hunting dog)
- Bat-eared fox
- Black-backed jackal (silverback jackal)
- Coyote
- Dingo (Australian wild dog)
- Fennec fox
- Grey wolf (timber or white wolf)
- Maned wolf (maned fox)
- Red fox

The dog family includes wolves, foxes and jackals as well as the domestic dog with its hundreds of breeds or varieties. Most foxes live alone but other dogs dwell in groups or packs, usually led by a chief male. They keep in touch and show their mood by barks, howls, whines, growls and many other noises. Cats may be stealthy sprinters, but dogs can run and trot all day on their long, powerful legs and eventually wear down their prey. All members of the group eat meat but many also take a wide range of other foods including grubs, worms, insects and berries. Domestic dogs were probably bred from the grey wolf thousands of years ago.

Grey wolf
Largest of the dog family, these wolves live in forest, scrub and mountains around the northern half of the world. They eat many foods, from deer to rabbits, mice, berries and fruits.

Black-backed jackal
These hardy jackals dwell in dry parts of east and southern Africa. They scavenge on zebras, antelopes and other large prey of big cats, and also kill smaller victims.

Fennec fox
This is the smallest fox. It lives in the Sahara Desert region, where it feeds mainly on ants, termites and other tiny prey. Its big ears help give off excess body warmth in the desert heat.

Maned wolf
The maned wolf's stilt-like legs give it a good view over the tall grasslands of South America. It searches at night for small animals and fruits.

Coyote
Coyotes are still common in some regions of North America, despite years of hunting. They can interbreed with grey wolves and also domestic dogs.

African wild dog
This fierce, large-fanged predator eats almost wholly meat. A pack of wild dogs can easily overpower a wildebeest or zebra.

Dingo
Dingoes may once have been part-domesticated. They now roam wild in the Australian bush. Unusually for dogs, they make hardly any sounds.

Bat-eared fox
This small African fox's huge ears locate its prey of large insects such as beetles and crickets. It can even hear dung-beetle maggots munching!

Red fox
Across Europe and North America the adaptable, clever red fox has taken to living in towns and even cities. It often raids dustbins, even in daylight.

One of the rarest members of the dog family is the African wild dog. There are only about 5000 left, mainly in one wildlife reserve in Tanzania.

Wolves, dogs and foxes

Far from cute and cuddly

▶ American black bear
▶ Asian black bear (Himalayan black bear)
▶ Brown bear (includes grizzly, Kodiak bear, Kamchatka bear, Alaskan bear)
▶ Sun bear (Malayan sun bear)
▶ Polar bear
▶ Sloth bear
▶ Spectacled bear

44

Bears may look amusing and cuddly, especially as 'teddy-bear' toys. But real bears are big, strong, powerful and sometimes very dangerous. They are best left alone. There are seven kinds of bears and they are all very similar. They have large heads, dog-like faces, big jaws, sharp teeth, bulky bodies, sturdy legs and very strong claws. Bears find meals mainly by smell. They like meat or fish but they also eat many other foods including fruits, berries and the honey of wild bees. Apart from the polar bear of the icy north, bears live in woods and forests. They are shy and rarely seen in the wild. They have also been hunted by people so most types are now rare.

Asian black bear
The Asian black bear has a jet-black coat of soft, silky fur with white markings on its chest. It also has larger, more rounded ears than other bears. It is an agile climber and often clambers into the branches to rest. This bear eats mainly fruit, nuts, shoots, grubs and insects, also birds and their eggs.

American black bear
This bear is found in North America, from Canada south to Mexico. Although some black bears really are black, others are brown, rusty-red, grey-blue or even creamy white. They like to stay in forests but they sometimes venture out to scavenge on dead farm animals or waste dumps.

Brown bear
Brown bears are found in woods and forests in Asia, North America and Europe. The largest types are the grizzly of North America and the Kodiak bear of Kodiak Island near Alaska. Europe's brown bears are smaller and now very rare, found only in a few isolated hills and mountain regions.

Polar bear
This bear's yellow-white fur blends with the snow and ice of its Arctic home. It helps the bear to creep up on its prey, mostly seals. It also hunts fish and swims well, the thick fur and blubber (fatty layer under the skin) keeping it warm in the freezing water. Some polar bears hang around towns and feed on scraps.

Sun bear
The smallest bear, at about 100 cm long, the sun bear of Southeast Asia lives in tropical forests. It feeds on shoots, fruits, birds, mice and other small animals. It also licks up termites.

Sloth bear
Eastern India and Sri Lanka are home to the unusual sloth bear with its long, shaggy fur. It often hangs upside down like a sloth using its long, curved claws.

Spectacled bear
The only bear from the southern half of the world, in South America, this type has pale markings around its eyes. It lives mainly in mountain forests.

The brown bear and polar bear are the largest meat-eating animals on land, even bigger than the Siberian tiger. A polar bear may be 3 m long and weigh 800 kg.

Scampering through the trees

▸ Coati
  (coati mundi)
▸ Giant panda
▸ Kinkajou
▸ Olingo
▸ Raccoon
▸ Red panda (lesser
  or red tree panda)

Raccoons, coatis, kinkajous and ringtails are agile, active creatures similar to dogs or small bears – except they live in trees. They are from the Americas, have long bodies and long tails and are active at night. Raccoons, especially, eat a huge variety of foods from small animals like mice, birds, frogs and fish to shoots, fruits and berries. Most have brown or grey fur, often with mask-like face markings and a ringed tail. Pandas are close cousins of raccoons from Asia. The red panda lives a similar lifestyle to the raccoon. However the giant panda eats bamboo and almost nothing else. It is very, very rare indeed – a world symbol of nature conservation.

Raccoon
Raccoons resemble burglar-masked, long-furred, bushy-tailed mini-bears. Like foxes they are well known as scavengers and often raid trash cans and rubbish heaps for leftover food scraps, usually at night. The raccoon holds its food delicately in its front paws for nibbling and may even wash it before eating.

Coati
Unlike most members of the raccoon group, coatis are usually active by day. They live in the forests of Central and South America. The coati uses its long, flexible nose to sniff out its food of insects and other small creatures from among leaves, rocks and bark. It also likes ripe fruits.

Olingo
The olingo's head and body are about 40 cm long – and so is its bushy tail, used for balancing among the branches. Olingos eat mostly fruits but they also take insects, birds and small mammals like mice. They gather with each other and with kinkajous for feeding trips and rarely come down to the ground.

Giant panda
There are fewer than 1000 giant pandas left in the wild, almost all in western China. They live alone in the thickest bamboo forests, eating the leaves and fleshy stems of these tall grasses. The panda has a 'sixth finger', which is really an extra-long wrist bone, to split open the bamboo shoots.

Red panda
Like a tree-living fox, the red panda has very soft reddish-brown fur. It is found in China, like its giant cousin, and also in nearby countries. It feeds on the ground on bamboo and other grasses, leaves, fruits and nuts, and it also catches small creatures. By day it sleeps in a tree, curled inside its bushy tail.

Kinkajou
One of the strangest members of the raccoon group, the kinkajou of Central and South America has short fur, large eyes and a prehensile or grasping tail. It can climb through trees almost as well as a monkey as it searches for fruits, the sweet nectar inside flowers and the honey of wild bees.

Bamboo is so poor in nutrients that the giant panda spends up to 16 hours each day eating. However if it comes across a dead animal, it helps itself to the rotting flesh.

Raccoons and pandas

Slinky killers

- American badger
- Chinese ferret-badger
- Eurasian badger
- Eurasian otter
- Ferret-polecat
- Little grison (Patagonian ferret)
- Marbled polecat (marbled ferret)
- Ratel (honey badger)
- Sea otter
- Speckle-necked otter (spot-necked otter)

Stoats, weasels, ferrets, polecats and martens are long-bodied, short-legged, sharp-toothed hunters. They are active, flexible and fast-moving and they often race into holes or burrows after prey. Many are extremely fierce, quite ready to attack animals larger than themselves. Otters and mink also belong to this mammal group, which is known as the mustelids. They swim well and prey on fish, crayfish and similar water creatures. Badgers and skunks are mustelids too. They catch small animals, especially earthworms and beetles. But badgers especially have a more varied range of foods and eat fruits, berries and other plant parts.

Ratel
The ratel is also known as the honey badger because it often feeds on the honey of wild bees – and their grubs too. It lives from Africa across the Middle East to India.

Eurasian badger
Badgers are very strong, powerful animals which come out at night. They live in family groups in a huge network of underground tunnels and chambers called a sett.

Sea otter
Sea otters rarely come onto land, and rarely go into water more than 15 m deep. They live along the coasts of the North and West Pacific and eat shellfish, worms, starfish and sea urchins.

Speckle-necked otter
This is probably the fastest and most skilful swimmer of all freshwater otters. It lives in rivers, lakes and swamps in most parts of Africa.

Chinese ferret-badger
Found across Southeast and East Asia, this animal can bite hard and produce a terrible smell when alarmed. It hunts mainly in trees.

Eurasian otter
The otter uses its webbed feet and strong, thick tail to swim speedily after food. It eats mainly fish but also hunts frogs, water voles and small waterbirds.

Little grison
This quick, darting predator is smaller than its cousin the grison from northern South America. The little grison lives in rocky mountains farther south.

American badger
Similar to its Eurasian cousin, the American badger has a dark cheek patch. It eats mainly rats, mice, voles, birds and birds' eggs.

Marbled polecat
The marbled polecat is small for a mustelid, with a head and body only 34 cm long. It lives across Central Asia and hunts mice, voles and lemmings.

The biggest otter is the giant or Brazilian otter of South American rivers and swamps. It grows to 2 m in total length and 30 kg in weight.

Polecats, otters and badgers

Clever cat-like killers

- African civet (African genet)
- African linsang
- Celebes palm civet (giant or brown palm civet)
- Giant genet
- Masked palm civet

Civets and genets are active hunters that look like a combination of cat and weasel. But they form their own mammal group, the viverrids, with about 35 species. Most are found in Africa or Southeast Asia, with the common genet ranging as far north as France. These stealthy predators have pointed faces and long tails, and many have striped or spotted fur. They hunt at night, often leaping through trees to seek out birds, lizards, squirrels, small monkeys and similar prey. Civets make a strong scent called musk. They mark out the boundaries of their territories with it, as a a sort of invisible signpost saying 'Keep out!' to others of their kind.

Giant genet
A secretive creature of the rainforests in Uganda and Zaire, the giant genet has heavily spotted fur. This type of pattern is called disruptive camouflage. It helps to break up the body outline as the genet slinks through the undergrowth, slipping in and out of the shadows and dappled patches of moonlight.

African civet
This is one of the larger viverrids, with a body and tail some 1.3 m long. Found across much of Africa, it is boldly marked and has a crest of raised hairs along the centre of its back and upper tail. Less of a climber than others in the group, it forages on the ground for small animals and occasionally fruit.

African linsang
This slender linsang is about the size of a pet cat. Indeed some linsangs, and especially genets, are kept as semi-tame pets which help to get rid of mice, rats and similar pests. The African linsang spends much time in trees, even building a nest there of twigs and leaves. Birds, lizards and insects make up most of its food.

Celebes palm civet
This very large and rare civet lives only on the island of Sulawesi (Celebes) in Southeast Asia. It is about 1.5 m in total length, including the tail, but is still at home in trees. Like cats, palm civets have retractile claws. This means they can be pulled into the toes to stay sharp.

Masked palm civet
This civet is grey or grey-brown all over except for its face markings. These have a mask-like pattern of black and white, resembling a badger, skunk or raccoon. Masked palm civets are found across a wide area from India east to China and south to Southeast Asia. People have also brought them to Japan. They have a mixed diet including mice, rats, insects and other small animals, and also plant shoots, soft roots and juicy fruits.

The similarity between the masked palm civet and the skunk goes further than face markings. The scent glands around the civet's rear end which produce the musk-based scent are large and their oily product is very strong-smelling. If threatened, the civet turns around and sprays this foul-smelling fluid at its attacker.

The powerful scent made by civets, called musk, was once collected and used as a basis for making fragrant perfumes.

Civets and genets

Superb swimmers of colder seas

▶ Caspian seal
▶ Common seal (harbour seal)
▶ Harp seal
▶ Ribbon seal
▶ Ringed seal

Seals are superbly equipped for life in water. Most live in oceans but a few, like the Caspian seal, dwell in large lakes and rivers. They swim by bending the body from side to side with a snake-like wriggling motion, the rear flippers working like a fish's tail to thrust the seal forwards. The front flippers trail by the sides of the body or are used for steering and braking. Seals are excellent divers – some types can stay under for more than 20 minutes. But on land they are clumsy and slow, humping along awkwardly. The 19 species of seals are found mainly in colder northern and southern waters and feed on fish, squid, shrimps and even seabirds.

52

Harp seal
A seal of the far north, in the North Atlantic and Arctic Ocean, harp seals rarely come to land. They spend most of their lives swimming or resting on icebergs. Their pups are even born on floating pack-ice. The young pups have soft, silky, pure white fur. The darker markings develop over the first few months.

Common seal
The common seal is one of the most familiar of all seals. It lives in all northern oceans, wandering as far south as the shores of France and Cape Cod in the Atlantic, and California and Japan in the Pacific. As the other name of harbour seal suggests, these seals tend to stay near land and are sometimes seen in ports and harbours and along holiday coasts. They can be inquisitive, coming to ships and quays to look for food. They also swim up rivers into lakes. The common seal is about 1.5–1.8 m in total length and weighs 90–120 kg, although as in other seals, males are slightly larger than females. They feed on fish, squid and shellfish and like other seals they are fairly long-lived, sometimes over 30 years.

Caspian seal
This small seal, about 1.2 m long, is found only in the huge inland saltwater lake called the Caspian Sea in Asia. It breeds on the pack-ice which forms there during the winter. When the water warms up in the spring the seals spread out. They spend most of their time fishing in deeper, cooler waters in the south of the lake.

Ribbon seal
These seals live mainly in the Bering Sea of the North Pacific, where they breed in early spring on the pack-ice. As summer arrives and the ice melts they roam in the open ocean far from land. They live in deeper water than other seals and dive far below the surface to hunt for fish, shrimps and squid.

Ringed seal
The ringed seal lives more on its own compared to other seals. It is found in northern seas and also freshwater lakes of Finland and Russia. It makes breathing holes in the ice as this forms in autumn, and keeps them open all winter. Seals have a thick layer of fatty blubber under the skin to keep them warm.

The ringed seal is one of the most common seals, with a world population of more than 5 million – far greater than the number of so-called 'common' seals!

Seals

Mysterious whales of the deep

- ▸ Baird's beaked whale (northern four-toothed whale)
- ▸ Cuvier's beaked whale (goose-beaked whale)
- ▸ Sowerby's beaked whale (North Sea beaked whale)
- ▸ Northern bottlenose whale

There are 18 different kinds or species of beaked whales, named after their bird-like beaked noses. Most are between 5 and 10 m long and look like a combination of great whale and dolphin. But they are mysterious and seldom-seen creatures and little is known about their lives. They spend most of their time far below the surface, diving to enormous depths. They probably swim close to the sea bed and follow underwater hills and valleys as they hunt squid, fish and similar victims. Beaked whales usually have marks and scratches over their backs. These may be the results of fights with their prey, or with breeding rivals of their own species.

Cuvier's beaked whale
In this beaked whale the nose 'beak' is quite short and the forehead is less bulbous than in other beaked whales. (The bulging foreheads of beaked whales led to their nickname of 'barrel-heads'.) Cuvier's beaked whale ranges widely through the world's seas. It reaches 7 m in length and 6 tonnes in weight. The white patches on its body are often caused by parasites such as fish-lice and barnacles growing on its skin. It is named after Baron Georges Cuvier, the great French scientist and fossil expert from the 1800s.

Baird's beaked whale
Sometimes known as the northern giant bottlenose, this alternative name gives a good idea of its appearance – similar to a giant version of the familiar bottlenosed dolphin. This is the largest beaked whale, growing to 12 m long and 13 tonnes in weight, although females are slightly larger than males. These elusive whales live in the waters of the North Pacific Ocean, descending more than 1000 m when hunting. They have just four teeth, each about 6–7 cm long, two on either side near the front of the lower jaw.

Northern bottlenose whale
This whale has the largest, most bulging forehead of the whole group. It lives in the deep waters of the North Atlantic, usually travelling about in small herds like other beaked whales. It can dive to 1000 m or more and stay underwater for two hours! Northern bottlenose whales migrate north towards the Arctic in spring and back to warmer waters in autumn. They are about 9–10 m long and 10 tonnes in weight when fully grown. Like most beaked whales they are long-lived, reaching perhaps 40 years of age.

Sowerby's beaked whale
This small beaked whale grows to 5 m long and is found mainly in the North Atlantic Ocean. It is occasionally stranded on European shores. Sowerby's beaked whale is a member of a sub-group of beaked whales which have just two teeth. These are quite large and grow towards the front of the lower jaw. All of these whales have them but the teeth only erupt, or grow out of the gum, in older individuals. Then the teeth can be seen protruding from the mouth. This whale dives to 2000 m and feeds mainly on squid.

Living specimens of one type of beaked whale, Shepherd's beaked whale, have only been seen about 10 times.

Beaked whales

The greatest creatures on Earth

▸ Blue whale
  (Sibbald's rorqual
  or sulphur-
  bottomed whale)
▸ Bowhead
  (Greenland right
  whale)
▸ Fin whale
▸ Grey whale (shown
  with calf, also
  group or pod of
  greys)
▸ Minke whale

There are 10 kinds of great or baleen whales. They are flesh-eaters but they have no teeth. Their huge mouths contain bristly, comb-shaped plates made of a springy, plastic-like substance, baleen. The plates hang like curtains from the roof of the mouth. The whale gulps in water, closes its mouth and pushes the water out with its tongue. The baleen works like a sieve to filter out small creatures – especially shrimp-like krill.

Blue whale
The blue is not only the largest whale, but also the largest mammal, and probably the biggest creature that ever lived. It can measure more than 30 m long and weigh 160 tonnes. It also eats 4 tonnes of krill each day in the rich summer seas around Antarctica. Blues migrate towards the tropics for winter.

Bowhead
The bowhead occurs in Arctic waters, especially the Bering Sea. It has still not recovered from the days of mass whaling and it may number only a few thousand. It has massive curving jaws, a huge gaping mouth and the longest, finest-fringed baleen plates of any whale, more than 4 m in length.

Grey whale
Grey whales dive as deep as 100 m to the ocean floor and plough their mouths through the mud to scoop up shellfish, worms and other sea-bed animals. Grey whales make the longest mammal migrations, up to 15,000 km between their winter breeding grounds off the Mexican coast and their summer waters of the Bering Sea.

Minke whale
Resembling a miniature blue whale, the minke is the smallest great whale at 'only' 11 m long. It has short baleen plates and catches squid and fish.

Fin whale
The fin whale is second only to the blue whale in size, at 25 m long and 80 tonnes in weight. It is found in all the world's oceans. Fin whales feed mostly at the surface or just below and they catch small fish and seabirds as well as krill. They are also the fastest of the great whales, powering along at speeds of more than 30 km/h for many hours.

The biggest animal baby is the blue whale calf. At birth it is more than 7 m long and 2 tonnes in weight. By the age of 7 months it weighs almost 25 tonnes.

Great whales

Huge eyes in the dark forest

▶ Golden potto (angwantibo)
▶ Lesser bushbaby
▶ Needle-clawed bushbaby
▶ Philippines tarsier
▶ Potto
▶ Slender loris
▶ Slow loris
▶ Thick-tailed bushbaby

They may look like big-eyed squirrels, and they have similar lives as they leap and bound through trees. But the bushbabies, pottos, lorises and tarsiers are active at night and they are in the primate group, related to lemurs, monkeys and apes. Like monkeys they have relatively large brains, well-developed hands with gripping thumbs, and large forward-facing eyes. Bushbabies live in Africa and catch insects using their sight and also their amazing hearing. Slower-moving are the lorises and pottos of Africa and Asia. They creep silently along branches as they sniff out their food of fruits, tree sap, insects, grubs and even the occasional small bird.

Thick-tailed bushbaby
This is the largest bushbaby with a nose-tail length of 75 cm. It lives in the forest and bush of East and Southern Africa and eats many foods including lizards and birds.

Needle-clawed bushbaby
This bushbaby's claws really are needle-sharp. Like other bushbabies it uses its long, fluffy tail to balance and turn in jumps.

Slow loris
Found in many parts of Southeast Asia, the slow loris 'freezes' when disturbed. It can remain completely still for an hour until its predator loses interest.

Slender loris
India and Sri Lanka are home to the slender loris. It eats many insects, even poisonous ones such as hairy caterpillars. It rubs off the stinging hairs before swallowing its prey.

Golden potto
This potto is a slow-moving creature of the night. It lives in the rainforests of Central Africa where it feeds mainly on maggots, caterpillars and similar grubs.

Potto
Resembling a teddy bear, the potto clambers along and underneath branches in the forests of Central Africa. It eats almost anything from sap to bats.

Philippines tarsier
Tarsiers are found only in Southeast Asia, including parts of the Philippines. They have huge eyes and very flexible necks, so the head can swivel almost all the way around like an owl. The tarsier sits still on its branch. When a lizard, mouse or insect ambles past it quickly pounces.

Lesser bushbaby
The commonest bushbaby, this type is found in many parts of Africa, mainly in drier woods and open bushland. Bushbabies keep in touch with each other by loud, twittering calls as they spring and leap through the trees at night. By day they sleep together, huddled in a tree hole or the crook of a branch.

Bushbabies are named after their child-like faces with large eyes, and also after their eerie wails at night which sound like a human baby crying.

Bushbabies, pottos, lorises and tarsiers

Monkeys with dog-like faces

▸ Black-and-white colobus (Angolan black colobus or white-epauletted colobus)
▸ Mandrill
▸ Moustached monkey
▸ Patas monkey
▸ Proboscis monkey

Monkeys are busy, active, agile, inquisitive creatures who live in groups, leap about in trees and make various whooping and screeching noises. The monkeys of Africa and Asia (Old World) do not have the grasping, prehensile tails of their American (New World) cousins. They also have longer muzzles with the nostrils close together so the face resembles a dog. But it can be a very colourful face, with fur or bare skin of glowing red, blue or yellow. The facial colours of full-grown adults usually become even brighter in the breeding season, showing that they are ready to mate. The backside or rump is often just as colourful, and for the same reason.

Moustached monkey
Like most monkeys the moustached monkey of West Africa is an 'opportunistic' feeder. This means it isn't a fussy eater. It consumes plant foods such as seeds, nuts, fruits, leaves, flowers and shoots. It also takes animal foods such as insects, grubs, lizards, birds' eggs and chicks – and anything else!

Black-and-white colobus
Familiar across the middle of Africa, black-and-white colobuses rarely come down to the ground. In the morning and evening they search for food in the tree tops. In the midday heat they relax and groom each other. The physical contact of grooming is important in keeping the group together.

Proboscis monkey
This rare monkey is named after its enormous nose, which is much bigger in the male. It lives only in the coastal mangrove swamps and riverbank trees of Borneo in Southeast Asia. It is a very specialist feeder, munching mainly on the leaves and fruits of mangrove and pedada trees.

Mandrill
This type of baboon lives in West African forests and, with its close relative the drill, is the biggest kind of monkey. A male mandrill has a head and body 90 cm long and weighs 50 kg. When it bares its fang-like canine teeth it is more than a match for leopards and other predators.

Patas monkey
Slim and long-legged, this African monkey can climb much better than a human and also run faster, reaching 50 km per hour! An old, experienced male leads his troop of about 10 females and their young. They feed by day on the ground, munching almost anything edible, and sleep at night in trees.

A MEAL WITH A FRIEND
Almost all kinds of monkeys live in groups, usually led by a mature, powerful male. Screeches and other calls are important to keep in contact. Grooming is too, and it also helps health. Troop members delicately pick fleas, lice and other pests from each other's fur and skin – and eat them.

In a well-fed proboscis monkey, one-third of the entire body weight is the stomach with the leaves inside.

Old World monkeys

Our closest cousins

▶ Chimpanzee
(common
chimpanzee)
▶ Gorilla
▶ Lar gibbon
(common or white-
handed gibbon)
▶ Orang (orang-
utan)
▶ Siamang
(black gibbon)

Apes are cousins of monkeys – and ourselves. An ape has a large head and brain relative to its body size, forward-facing eyes, front limbs longer than back limbs, and no tail. There are two main ape groups. The great apes include just four species – the orang of Southeast Asia, and the gorilla, common chimp and pygmy chimp (bonobo), all of Africa. Their hands have very moveable thumbs that can grip and manipulate. The lesser apes are called gibbons. There are nine species, all found in the forests of Southeast Asia. Gibbons are incredibly agile climbers. They swing through the branches using their long, muscular arms.

62

Orang
Orangs live only in the thick forests of Sumatra and Borneo. They are rare, shy and seldom seen. Their bright reddish-brown fur grows long and shaggy with age. Orangs spend many hours feasting on soft fruits such as figs and mangos. They also eat leaves, shoots, nuts, soft bark and occasionally small animals.

Lar gibbon
The fur of the lar gibbon varies across its wide range of Thailand, Malaysia and Sumatra, from black in some areas to buff, brown or red in other regions. But its hands and face-ring are always white. Gibbons eat mainly ripe fruits, also soft leaves and soft-bodied animals such as insect grubs.

Gorilla
The huge and muscular gorilla is a peaceful animal which eats almost entirely plant food. Gorillas live in small family groups in the dense African forest, feeding mainly on leaves and stems. They spend most of their time on the ground. At night they generally sleep in tree nests made by bending branches together.

Siamang
With a head-body length of almost 100 cm, this is the largest gibbon. It inhabits the forests of Malaysia and Sumatra. The male and female make loud calls and often sing together in a 'duet'. Unusually for a mammal, when the baby siamang is about one year old, the father takes over from the mother and looks after it.

Chimpanzee
Although called the 'common' chimpanzee, this ape is becoming scarce in its natural habitat – the savannahs, bush and forests of Central Africa. Chimps face destruction of their home areas and illegal trapping for the trade in exotic pets. They are mainly plant-eaters but also take some animals, especially termites, ants and certain kinds of caterpillars. Occasionally young adult male chimps from a troop form a 'hunting party'. They chase after and kill a larger prey such as a monkey, bird, small deer or even a chimp from a neighbouring troop. A baby chimp can do little except cling to its mother and feed on her milk. As it grows it begins to play with other youngsters in the troop. But it stays with its mother for 6–7 years.

A large male gorilla grows to 1.9 m tall, weighs up to 200 kg, and is as strong as three adult humans.

Greater and lesser apes

Index

A

Aardvark 24–25
African bush squirrel 18–19
African civet 50–51
African elephant 24–25
African genet 50–51
African linsang 50–51
African pygmy mouse 14–15
African wild ass 26–27
African wild dog 42–43
African yellow-winged bat 12–13
Alaskan bear 44–45
Alpaca 34–35
American badger 48–49
American black bear 44–45
Andean tapir 28–29
Angolan black colobus 60–61
anteater,
  Banded 8–9
  Collared 22–23
  Giant 22–23
  Silky 22–23
  Tree 22–23
  Two-toed 22–23
Arabian camel 34–35
armadillo,
  Burmeister's 22–23
  Common long-nosed 22–23
  Fairy 22–23
  Naked-tailed 22–23
  Nine-banded 22–23
Asian black bear 44–45
Asian camel 34–35
Asian elephant 24–25
Asian two-horned rhinoceros 30–31
Asiatic striped palm squirrel 18–19
Asiatic wild ass 26–27
ass,
  African wild 26–27
  Asiatic wild 26–27
Australian wild dog 42–43

B

Baboon 60
Bactrian camel 34–35
badger,
  American 48–49
  Eurasian 48–49
  Honey 48–49
Baird's beaked whale 54–55
Baird's tapir 28–29
Banded anteater 8–9
Baringo giraffe 32–33
Barrel-head whale 54–55
bat,
  African yellow-winged 12–13
  Hammer-headed 12–13
  Hoary 12–13
  Horse-headed 12–13
  Lesser horseshoe 12–13
  Long-eared 12–13
  Mexican fishing 12–13
  Mexican free-tailed 12–13
  Noctule 12–13
  Red 12–13
  Spotted 12–13
Bat-eared fox 42–43
bear,
  Alaskan 44–45
  American black 44–45
  Asian black 44–45
  Brown 44–45
  Grizzly 44–45
  Himalayan black 44–45
  Kamchatka 44–45
  Kodiak 44–45
  Malayan sun 44–45
  Polar 44–45
  Sloth 44–45
  Spectacled 44–45
  Sun 44–45
Beaver 18–19
beavers 16
Beisa oryx 36–37

big cats 38, 40
Black gibbon 62–63
Black rat 14–15
Black rhinoceros 30–31
Black-and-white colobus 60–61
Black-backed jackal 42–43
Black-tailed jackrabbit 20–21
Blesbok 36–37
Blue whale 56–57
Blue wildebeest 36–37
Bontebok 36–37
Bowhead 56–57
Brazilian badger 48–49
Brazilian tapir 28–29
Brindled gnu 36–37
Brindled wildebeest 36–37
Brown bear 44–45 ·
Brown hare 20–21
Brown palm civet 50–51
Brown rat 14–15
Brush-tailed phascogale 8–9
Burchell's zebra 26–27
Burmeister's armadillo 22–23
bushbaby,
  Lesser 58–59
  Needle-clawed 58–59
  Thick-tailed 58–59
Bush-tailed ground squirrel 18–19

C

camel,
  Arabian 34–35
  Asian 34–35
  Bactrian 34–35
  One-humped 34–35
  Two-humped 34–35
Cape hunting dog 42–43
Capybara 16–17
Caspian seal 52–53
Caspian tiger 40–41
Cavy 16–17
Celebes palm civet 50–51
Chapman's zebra 26–27
Cheetah 38–39
Chimpanzee 62–63
  Common 62–63
Chinchilla 16–17
Chinese ferret-badger 48–49
civet,
  African 50–51
  Brown palm 50–51
  Celebes palm 50–51
  Giant palm 50–51
  Masked palm 50–51
Clouded leopard 38–39
Coati (Coati mundi) 46–47
Collared anteater 22–23
colobus,
  Angolan black 60–61
  Black-and-white 60–61
  White-epauletted 60–61
Common chimpanzee 62–63
Common gibbon 62–63
Common hare 20–21
Common long-nosed armadillo 22–23
Common marmot 18–19
Common rabbit 20–21
Common seal 52–53
Common wambenger 8–9
Common zebra 26–27
Cony 20–21
Coyote 42–43
Coypu 16–17
Crested porcupine 16–17
Cuvier's beaked whale 54–55

D

Desert jerboa 14–15
desman, Pyrenean 10–11
devil, Tasmanian 8–9
Dingo 42–43
dog,
  African wild 42–43
  Australian wild 42–43
  Cape hunting 42–43
Donkey 26–27

Drill 60
Dromedary 34–35

E

elephant,
  African 24–25
  Asian 24–25
elephants 32
Eurasian badger 48–49
Eurasian otter 48–49
Eurasian red squirrel 18–19
European hedgehog 10–11
European mole 10–11
European rabbit 20–21

F

Fairy armadillo 22–23
Fennec fox 42–43
ferret,
  Marbled 48–49
  Patagonian 48–49
ferret-badger, Chinese 48–49
Ferret-polecat 48–49
Fin whale 56–57
fox,
  Bat-eared 42–43
  Fennec 42–43
  Maned 42–43
  Red 42–43

G

Gemsbok 36–37
genet,
  African 50–51
  Giant 50–51
Gerenuk 36–37
Giant anteater 22–23
Giant genet 50–51
Giant palm civet 50–51
Giant panda 46–47
gibbon,
  Black 62–63
  Common 62–63
  Lar 62–63
  White-handed 62–63
giraffe,
  Baringo 32–33
  Masai 32–33
  Nubian 32–33
  Reticulated 32–33
  Transvaal 32–33
gnu, Brindled 36–37
Golden potto 58–59
Goose-beaked whale 54–55
Gorilla 62–63
Greater one-horned rhinoceros 30–31
Greenland right whale 56–57
Grevy's zebra 26–27
Grey whale 56–57
Grey wolf 42–43
grison 48
Grizzly bear 44–45
Guanaco 34–35
guinea pig,
  pet 16
  Wild 16–17

H

Hairy-nosed wombat 8–9
Hammer-headed bat 12–13
Harbour seal 52–53
hare,
  Common 20–21
  Mountain 20–21
  Snowshoe 20–21
  Tundra 20–21
  Varying 20–21
Harp seal 52–53
Harvest mouse 14–15
hedgehog, European 10–11
Himalayan black bear 44–45
Hippopotamus 32–33
  Pygmy 32–33
Hispaniolan solenodon 10–11
Hoary bat 12–13
Honey badger 48–49
Hook-lipped rhinoceros 30–31
horse, Przewalski's 26–27
Horse-headed bat 12–13
horses 26–27
House mouse 14–15

Hutia 16–17
Hyaena 40
hyrax, Rock 24–25

I

Indian giant squirrel 18–19
Indian rhinoceros 30–31
Indian tiger 40–41
Indo-Chinese tiger 40
insectivores 10

J

jackal 40
  Black-backed 42–43
  Silverback 42–43
Jaguar 38–39
Javan rhinoceros 30–31
jerboa,
  Desert 14–15
  Three-toed 14–15

K

Kamchatka bear 44–45
kangaroo, Red 8–9
Kiang 26
Kinkajou 46–47
Klipspringer 36–37
Kodiak bear 44–45

L

Lar gibbon 62–63
Large-eared pika 20–21
Least shrew 10–11
leopard,
  Clouded 38–39
  Snow 38–39
Lesser bushbaby 58–59
Lesser horseshoe bat 12–13
Lesser one-horned rhinoceros 30–31
Lesser panda 46–47
linsang, African 50–51
Lion 38–39
Little grison 48–49
Llama 34–35
Long-eared bat 12–13
loris,
  Slender 58–59
  Slow 58–59
Lowland tapir 28–29

M

Malabar giant squirrel 18–19
Malayan sun bear 44–45
Malaysian tapir 28–29
Mandrill 60–61
Maned fox 42–43
Maned wolf 42–43
Marbled ferret 48–49
Marbled polecat 48–49
marmot, Common 18–19
martens 48
Masai giraffe 32–33
Masked palm civet 50–51
Mexican fishing bat 12–13
Mexican free-tailed bat 12–13
mice, pocket 16
Mink 48
Minke whale 56–57
mole, European 10–11
monkey,
  Moustached 60–61
  Patas 60–61
  Proboscis 60–61
monkeys,
  New World 60
  Old World 60–61
moonrats 10
Mountain hare 20–21
Mountain tapir 28–29
Mountain zebra 26–27
mouse,
  African pygmy 14–15
  Harvest 14–15
  House 14–15
  Rock 14–15
  Spiny 14–15
  Striped field 14–15
  Wood 14–15
  Yellow-necked field 14–15
Moustached monkey 60–61
mundi, Coati 46–47
mustelids 48

N

Naked-tailed armadillo 22–23

Needle-clawed bushbaby 58–59
New World monkeys 60
Nine-banded armadillo 22–23
Noctule bat 12–13
North American porcupine 16–17
North Sea beaked whale 54–55
Northern bottlenose whale 54–55
Northern flying squirrel 18–19
Northern four-toothed whale 54–55
Northern giant bottlenose whale 54–55
Northern pika 20–21
Norway rat 14–15
Nubian giraffe 32–33
Numbat 8–9

O

Okapi 32–33
Old World monkeys 60–61
Olingo 46–47
Onager 26
One-humped camel 34–35
Orang-utan 62–63
oryx,
  Beisa 36–37
  Scimitar 36–37
  White 36–37
otter,
  Brazilian 48
  Eurasian 48–49
  Sea 48–49
  Speckle-necked (Spot-necked) 48–49
Ounce 38–39

P

pademelon, Red-legged 8–9
panda,
  Giant 46–47
  Lesser 46–47
  Red (Red tree) 46–47
pangolin, Small-scaled tree 22–23
Patagonian ferret 48–49
Patas monkey 60–61
phascogale, Brush-tailed 8–9
Philippines tarsier 58–59
Pichi 22–23
pika,
  Large-eared 20–21
  Northern 20–21
  Red 20–21
  Steppe 20–21
Plains zebra 26–27
pocket mice 16
Polar bear 44–45
polecat, Marbled 48–49
porcupine,
  Crested 16–17
  North American 16–17
  South American 16–17
Potto 58–59
  Golden 58–59
Proboscis monkey 60–61
Pronghorn 36–37
Przewalski's horse 26–27
Pygmy hippopotamus 32–33
Pygmy shrew 10–11
pygmy voles 16
Pyrenean desman 10–11

QR

Quokka 8–9
Rabbit 20–21
  Common 20–21
  European 20–21
Raccoon 46–47
rat,
  Black 14–15
  Brown 14–15
  Norway 14–15
  Ship 14–15
  Water 14–15
Ratel 48–49
rats 16
Red bat 12–13
Red fox 42–43
Red kangaroo 8–9
Red-legged pademelon 8–9
Red panda 46–47
Red pika 20–21

Red tree panda 46–47
Reticulated giraffe 32–33
rhinoceros,
  Asian two-horned 30–31
  Black 30–31
  Greater one-horned 30–31
  Hook-lipped 30–31
  Indian 30–31
  Javan 30–31
  Lesser one-horned 30–31
  Square-lipped 30–31
  Sumatran 30–31
  White 30–31
rhinos 26
Ribbon seal 52–53
ringtails 46–47
Rock hyrax 24–25
Rock mouse 14–15
rodents 14, 16
rorqual, Sibbald's 56–57
Rufous elephant shrew 10–11

S

Sable 36–37
Sassaby 36–37
Scimitar oryx 36–37
Sea otter 48–49
seal,
  Caspian 52–53
  Common 52–53
  Harbour 52–53
  Harp 52–53
  Ribbon 52–53
  Ringed 52–53
Shepherd's beaked whale 54–55
Ship rat 14
shrew,
  Least 10–11
  Pygmy 10–11
  Rufous elephant 10–11
Siamang 62–63
Siberian tiger 40–41, 44
Silky anteater 22–23
Silverback jackal 42–43
skunks 48
Slender loris 58–59
Sloth bear 44–45
Slow loris 58–59
Small-scaled tree pangolin 22–23
Snow leopard 38–39
Snowshoe hare 20–21
solenodon, Hispaniolan 10–11
South American porcupine 16–17
South American tapir 28–29
Sowerby's beaked whale 54–55
Spanish giant donkey 26–27
Speckle-necked otter 48–49
Spectacled bear 44–45
Spiny mouse 14–15
Spot-necked otter 48–49
Spotted bat 12–13
Square-lipped rhinoceros 30–31
squirrel,
  African bush 18–19
  Asiatic striped palm 18–19
  Bush-tailed ground 18–19
  Eurasian red 18–19
  Indian giant 18–19
  Malabar giant 18–19
  Northern flying 18–19
squirrels 16
Steppe pika 20–21
stoats 48
Striped field mouse 14–15
Sulphur-bottomed whale 56–57
Sumatran rhinoceros 30–31
Sumatran tiger 40–41
Sun bear 44–45

T

Tamandua 22–23
tapir,
  Andean 28–29
  Baird's 28–29
  Brazilian 28–29

Lowland 28–29
Malaysian 28–29
Mountain 28–29
South American 28–29
Woolly 28–29
tapirs 26
tarsier, Philippines 58–59
Tasmanian devil 8–9
tenrecs 10
Thick-tailed bushbaby 58–59
Three-toed jerboa 14–15
tiger 38
  Caspian 40–41
  Indian 40–41
  Indo-Chinese 40
  Siberian 40–41, 44
  Sumatran 40–41
  White Indian 40–41
Timber wolf 42–43
Topi 36–37
Transvaal giraffe 32–33
Tree anteater 22–23
Tundra hare 20–21
Two-humped camel 34–35
Two-toed anteater 22–23

UV

ungulates 26
Varying hare 20–21
Vicuna 34–35
viverrids 50
voles, pygmy 16

W

wallaby, Yellow-footed rock 8–9
wambenger, Common 8–9
Water rat 14–15
weasels 48
whale,
  Baird's beaked 54–55
  Barrel-head 54–55
  Blue 56–57
  Cuvier's beaked 54–55
  Fin 56–57
  Goose-beaked 54–55
  Greenland right 56–57
  Grey 56–57
  Minke 56–57
  North Sea beaked 54–55
  Northern bottlenose 54–55
  Northern four-toothed 54–55
  Northern giant bottlenose 54–55
  Shepherd's beaked 54–55
  Sowerby's beaked 54–55
  Sulphur-bottomed 56–57
  White-epauletted colobus 60–61
White-handed gibbon 62–63
White Indian tiger 40–41
White oryx 36–37
White rhinoceros 30–31
White wolf 42–43
Wild guinea pig 16–17
wildebeest,
  Blue 36–37
  Brindled 36–37
wolf,
  Grey 42–43
  Maned 42–43
  Timber 42–43
  White 42–43
wombat, Hairy-nosed 8–9
Wood mouse 14–15
Woolly tapir 28–29

Y

Yellow-footed rock wallaby 8–9
Yellow-necked field mouse 14–15

Z

zebra,
  Burchell's 26–27
  Chapman's 26–27
  Common 26–27
  Grevy's 26–27
  Mountain 26–27
  Plains 26–27